Quick Guide to Networking, Social Media and Social Capital

Liz Broomfield

ISBN: 1508761345

ISBN-13: 978-1508761341

DEDICATION

To Matthew, as always

CONTENTS

ACKNOWLEDGEMENTS

Many thanks to Linda Bates for beta reading, Catherine Fitzsimons for editing and my husband, Matthew Dexter, for letting me create social media profiles in his name and for all the cups of tea.

INTRODUCTION

Welcome to this guide to networking, social media and social capital!

Why have I put these three topics together? Because social media networks and the physical networks inherent in networking groups are very similar and can all do the same thing: raise your social capital, which is something you can bank and 'spend' when you need publicity, favours or promotion.

But it's not all a one-way street, standing around shouting about your business and demanding that other people do that, too. I firmly believe that social media and networking are all about sharing, about helping other people, about putting people together, introducing people who might never have met before, and as a side effect, possibly finding that people help you, too.

All a bit corporate sounding and scary for you? Networking, both in the flesh and via social media platforms like Twitter, Facebook, LinkedIn and Google+, doesn't have to be all business and no fun – and it certainly doesn't have to be suited, booted, covered in make-up or sporting a club tie. The important thing is to choose to interact with the groups and people who suit you, who are like you, who are in the same line of business and who can act as a mutual support team.

In this guide, I'm going to:

Show you how networking does NOT have to be scary, with some tips and hints to help you relax and even enjoy yourself!

Explain what social media is and how you can use the most common platforms to make friends and contacts, get exposure for your business and, most importantly, go about things in the right (and polite) way

Tell you a little bit about blogging and how that can work to link your social media platforms and share your (and others') messages

Explain what social capital is, how you build it and how you can take advantage of it

Why you should buy this book

You should buy this book if you want to find out more about using social media and physical networks to grow your influence and business.

Why you shouldn't buy this book

If you're looking for a more general book on growing your business, you would do better to have a look at my other business books: find out more at www.lizbroomfieldbooks.com.

If you already have my second business book, "Running a Successful Business After the Start-up Phase", or my business omnibus, "Your Guide to Starting and Running your Business", then lots of the information in this quick guide is covered there. I don't want to rip you off, so if you've already bought this book expecting a lot of new material, please feel free to return it to Amazon for a refund.

Although I give you lots of hints on networking and marketing, if you're looking for a book about network marketing (think Amway and Forever Living) this one is not specifically on that topic; such companies have particular ways of operating and are not what I'm talking about here.

Now we've got that straight, let's look at how to use this guide!

How to use this guide

Many people still read e-books like this one on their Kindle. To make it as easy to read as possible, I've not included images, screenshots and diagrams.

What I have done is included links to FREE resources on my blog. There is no sign-up needed, I'm not going to harvest your email address, and you're not going to find yourself signed up to a newsletter you can't escape.

The posts I link to at the start of each section have screenshots and detailed step-by-step instructions for setting up and working with the platforms and programs I talk about in this guide. Do take advantage of these and click through where I alert you that there's a link, or make a note of the URL if you're not on Wi-Fi at the time.

There's also a resource guide at the end of this book with the full URLs for all of the resources I mention in the text.

If you want to find all of my social media resources in one place, pop over to my blog resource guide at http://libroediting.com/blog/students-small-businesses-word-users/ for more screenshots and diagrams than you could ever need!

I hope you enjoy this short guide. You can read it straight through or pick out the sections that are most useful to you. Don't forget to look at the free online resources too!

NETWORKING

Physical networking, where you walk into a room full of people and chat to them about business (tea, cats, clothes …) is something people are always pushing at you when you're new to business. It can be a bit scary, but here's the thing: pretty everyone will say they dislike it and are scared of it.

It can't be that bad, can it? No. I'm what's called an introvert (I gain my strength and energy from time spent alone rather than from time spent with people) and I can be quite shy, but there's a lot to be said for giving it a go (a few times) even if you only pop in to an event for 10 minutes and promise yourself you can run away after that.

Here are my tips on Networking for Newbies and some thoughts on the similarities between physical networking (in rooms full of people with a daunting coffee machine in the corner) and social media networking online.

Networking for Newbies

Networking can be a scary and daunting idea. We all know we need to do it ... but how, where and why do we do it? What can we get out of it, and bring to it? Here are 10 handy hints for making networking work for you, all tested by me, myself – and I certainly didn't think I was a natural networker when I started out!

Do be scared ... but realise everyone else is too!
Walking into a room full of people you don't know is daunting to all but the most extrovert of people. The key to conquering this fear is knowing that 90% of the people around you, even people who have been to the event before, are at least a little apprehensive, too. So, first of all, be understanding if people seem a bit aggressive or over-wordy or, indeed, silent. Maybe it's just how they are when they're nervous. And secondly, let yourself off the hook if you do the same. Take a deep calming breath, look around you and chat to someone. Ask them about themselves – age-old advice, but it does really work.

Dress for success
You don't always need to be all suited and booted, but it's worth finding out from the event organiser what kind of outfits people normally turn up in (of course, "what you usually wear to work" isn't always suitable if you normally work from a home office ...). Most of us feel more comfortable when we fit in with the crowd, and knowing how to pitch your outfit is part of that. It goes without saying – doesn't it? that you should be ironed and mud-free and your hair shouldn't be standing on end unless it's supposed to.

Try before you buy
There's a huge variety of networking events and organisations out there. Some of them charge a fee to be a member of their club. That's fine. But most of them will let you try out a meeting or two before you commit to that expensive membership. Take advantage of this, try a few different local meetings before you join up, and you'll know you've spent your money in the right place.

Diversify
The huge range of networking events available means that there's one – or more – to suit everyone. From a national organisation to a hyperlocal event, from market sector themed meetings to Women in Business, try out a few and see what you like – and try to visit a range of different ones every month. Of course, there are also online networking groups, forums, LinkedIn groups, etc. Give those a go, by all means, but do try and get out and about –

especially if you work alone all day! If you're chatting to someone at a networking event and you seem to get on and have similar views, ask them which other meetings they go to. Other ways to find out more include social networks, including meetup.com, Facebook and Twitter, notices in your local library, and articles in business magazines. People are usually fine to tell you about the other ones they go to and might even arrange to meet up with you first to take the edge off that first entrance into the room.

Go local
I joined my local High Street Business Association. I've got a small ad on their website and a listing in their directory and I go to breakfast meetings at a local café. You've always got something to talk about when you're all local! And you might be able to help your local community too, with fund-raising events or supporting Business Enterprise Zones and mentoring schemes.

Keep at it
Most networking events happen regularly and some take a while to work your way in to. Some might have different attendees every time, some might have lots of familiar faces every month, and some might have a mix of the two. I'd suggest that you need a little time to get used to the particular group and how it works so do go more than once – plus, repeat appearances will keep you in people's minds.

Don't expect to make direct sales: do expect to get recommendations

You may well not sell your services to the people you meet at a networking event. Sometimes you might even meet a rival business owner who – gasp – does the same as you! Just because you're not going to get a sale doesn't mean you shouldn't talk to these people. You can talk about general business matters, get all sorts of tips and hints … and you don't know who they know. I've won a few clients through people I've met at networking events. One lady recommended me to a contact on Twitter, after I'd met her at a Social Media Café. It's always worth actually asking people to think of you if they come across anyone who needs whatever it is you do.

Do team up with "rivals"

I have a small network of other editors who I can rely on and, if I've got too much to do, I pass work on to them. Similarly, they pass work to me or recommend me if one of their clients comes to them with something in which I specialise. So if you meet someone who's in a similar line of business to you, don't bristle and walk away, but think how you can benefit one another.

Connect people

Don't just think about what you can get out of these events. If you meet enough different people, chances are that you'll meet someone who needs something and realise you know just the person that can help them. If they're both at the event, take the time to introduce them. They'll both thank you for it – and remember you. At a recent networking event, a local film-maker I've known for a while described me (in front of a group of other people) as an "oracle" and made sure everyone knew how I was always introducing him to interesting and useful people. Great word-of-mouth marketing!

Follow up
You will undoubtedly come back from networking events with a fistful of business cards. Don't just shove them in your filing cabinet, your pocket, or your handbag (or manbag!). Get them all out when you get back home, and go through them. Email everyone you met, even if you don't think you'll get a direct sale from them, to say that you enjoyed meeting them, and establish that contact. You never know when one of you might come in useful to the other one.

Do give networking a go – more than one go, in fact, so you can get used to how it all works. In no time, you'll be striding confidently in to the room, greeting familiar faces, making other people feel comfortable, and making useful contacts and/or helping other people.

Networking in Person and Networking via Social Media

Now we've learned a bit about real-life networking, let's talk about how social media and live networking are similar in so many ways. Here are some hints about how they work and how you can also help fellow businesses to use them.

Whether I'm talking to an individual at a networking event, tweeting a link to a blog post or updating my status on my business Libro's Facebook page, I'm (hopefully) addressing two audiences. The first is the person I'm speaking to. And the second is the people to whom they could potentially carry my message.

Networking events, co-working sessions, Twitter followers, Facebook friends – what they have in common is that each is a network. Think of it like pyramid selling or chain letters but in a good way. X knows 2 people who know 2 people each, that's 4, each of those know two people and that makes 8 – even if some of them know each other, the network doubles each time. Like rabbits …

These networks are more diverse and varied than you might at first think. Even if you're close to someone in your life, history or profession, it is unlikely that your network overlaps with theirs completely. Some examples:

My husband, who I've known since 2001 – only half of his friends are shared with me.

A Birmingham friend interested in the same things as me and in a few of the same friendship and interest groups – we have twice as many individual friends as we have shared ones.

An old University friend who is a freelancer like me has just 9 mutual friends out of a total joint friendship circle of over 700 people.

Similarly, way less than half of the people liking my Libro business page are personal friends of mine, and about a third of my friends have liked my business page, so the overlap isn't massive there.

It's the same on Twitter – I'm pretty sure that not all my friends' followers are following me (although it's harder to extract the figures there), so if I retweet a business's message, my 1,900 followers will see their message, and if they retweet mine, theirs will know about me.

When I'm at a networking meeting, I'm aware that the person I'm talking to is not always likely to want to buy my services. But it's very likely that, if I've made a good impression on them, they will remember me, and when they come across someone else in their social or business network who needs something that I offer, they will recall my details and pass my information on. There's lots of research on how to ensure that happens, but stick with the general principle that you may not get a job from the person you're talking to, but you may well from someone they know.

In the same way, if I tweet or put up a Facebook update about something Libro's doing, the people who see it directly from me probably know all about what I do, or they might not need a proofreader or transcriber right now. But if they share the Facebook post or retweet the tweet, who's to know who out of their wider circle might find it useful?

Much of my work comes through personal recommendation, usually from previous clients, but also through networks of friends and associates, and this is a general reflection on how you can help your friends with businesses small and not-so-small to grow their networks and get known about. Even large organisations need this – I was talking to someone from a museum just the other day, and he was bemoaning the lack of likes and shares on their Facebook page. Which is, by the way, good, engaging and interesting.

Hopefully this section has made you more aware of just how important the power of networks can be to your business. Remember it works the other way, too, so be kind and share: share a post or a tweet by a friend, a charity you support, a business you like … and someone in your network of contacts might find just what they need!

SOCIAL MEDIA

In each of the following sections on the different kinds of social media platform you can use, I include a guide to how to be polite and maintain reciprocity so as to "leverage your social capital" which actually just means make social media work for you and use sharing and friendliness to help yourself and others (see the last chapter in this book for more on social capital).

It's all about **reciprocity**. What does that mean?

The dictionary definition of reciprocity is – gaining mutual benefit from exchanging things with other people.

In the case of social media, in which I include blogging, done well it should be a two-way and mutual activity. This means building strands of connection which can, over time, turn into powerful networks that can help you start, grow or develop your business or other endeavour.

By responding to comments and forging links, sharing and re-tweeting, you make yourself more prominent in other people's eyes, *for the right reasons*.

If you are unfailingly polite, share people's content, always say thank you, share people's details with other people and act as an ambassador and connector for other people's personal brands as well as your own, that will come back to you in bucketfuls.

Whether you're just starting out, embracing a new form of social media, or need a gentle reminder (I know that writing this reminded me to return to sharing more on Twitter), I hope you find these tips useful.

ALL ABOUT FACEBOOK

Facebook for business – starting out

Find screen prints and full instructions for setting up your business Facebook page in this free resource on my blog (hover over the link to view and click, or have a look at the resource guide for full web addresses).

Setting up your Facebook page

You can set up a page for your business on Facebook as long as you've got a personal page and you're logged in at the time.

The slight issue with Facebook business pages is that Facebook wants you to pay for adverts and to have your posts and page promoted to other people. So do be prepared to receive lots of suggestions to pay for ads and promotion, and not a lot of interaction from other users.

Go to www.facebook.com/pages/create or click on **Create a page** when you're in any other Facebook page and choose a category of page to create.

If you choose **Local Business or Place**, or **Company**, **Organization** or **Institution**, you then need to choose your category, and it's worth noting that you get different categories for Local Businesses and Companies

Give your page a name. If you choose **Local Business or Place**, you're given space to enter your address – good if you have a shop or need people to find you, not really recommended if you operate from your home office and don't want all and sundry to know your address.

Whatever type of page you set up, you will be asked to tick that you accept Facebook's Page terms and conditions. These include a host of stipulations about promotions, advertising, tagging and other issues. Note that Facebook can remove admin rights and shut down your page if you don't abide by these rules. This is why I would never suggest limiting your web presence to only a Facebook page – make sure that you have your own website, too.

Now it's time to set up the basic details of your page – Facebook walks you through this:

Once you've said that it's a real organisation, you'll get a second option to confirm that you represent the company.

You can choose a URL for your page that includes the business name. Facebook checks that the URL you've chosen is available. (Note here that you used to have to have a certain number of Likes before you could choose a unique Facebook web address; now you can do it right away).

Once you've saved this information, you can add a profile photo, which you can upload from your computer (you'll be taken to your computer's folders to find the photo you want) or load from Facebook.

You will also be prompted to add the page to your favourites – this means that you'll see when you (or someone else) posts to it and you will also see it in your left-hand side panel.

Then you get a bit of hard sell with the **Reach More People** section. I would certainly advise pressing the **Skip button** at this point, as anyone directed by an ad to Like a page that has no Likes or activity is not going to be compelled to do so!

And now you have your page! You'll see a **Page button** at the top of the screen which allows you to return to it at any time.

Once you've set up your basic page, you can set up a cover image. There are all sorts of rules about what you can have here, but they change frequently, so refer to the current terms and conditions.

Choose a photo from your Facebook albums or upload one from your computer. Once you have uploaded the photo, you can move it around until it's in the right place, then **Save Changes**.

You can always change your profile picture and cover image in the future, by hovering over them, at which point a button will appear offering you the opportunity to do so.

You can now add information and details as you wish. Use the **Settings button** to access these options:

The **Settings pages** allow you to describe your business and add hours of operation, etc. You don't have to fill in everything, but it is useful to add your website's URL, for example. You can change this information at any time.

The **General section** also allows you to set out who can post on the page and other features. This is useful if you have people putting spam comments, etc., on the page – you can set it so that only you can post. However, I do like to let people post and comment to foster a sense of community. It's worth looking at this area frequently, as what you can and can't do does change over time.

Page Roles allows you to add other people who can administrate the page – useful if you've set up the page but you have someone in your company who's a social media expert. You can find full instructions on how to do this on the Libro blog.[1]

The **Activity tab** lets you know how often your posts have been seen and the viewing figures. Note that these are likely to be distressingly small – see the section on paying for promotion below.

---

[1] http://libroediting.com/2014/06/04/how-to-add-an-admin-or-moderator-to-your-facebook-business-page/

If you're considering paying for promotion on Facebook

Whenever I get tempted to advertise on Facebook, which they do promise can be targeted to your selected audience, I think about the random / odd / offensive / inappropriate adverts that I see on my Facebook timeline, and that makes me think that it's perhaps not worth it.

If you do decide to pay for advertising, go for one of the pay per click options where you can limit how much you pay out per day. Observe how it goes very carefully, and try to assess how much business you're actually getting for what you pay for (there's more on investing in your business in my book, "Running a Successful Business after the Start-up Phase").

Interacting with people on your page

You can post updates on your page, including photos and notes, just like you can on your personal Facebook timeline. I send my blog post notifications to this page – but then I share them to my personal timeline, too, where they have more chance of being seen.

When you **Like** a page belonging to someone else, you can click on the down-arrow by **Message** and **Like as your page** – this will appear in their timeline and can lead to some nice, friendly interaction.

If you have set your page up to accept comments by others, do pop by the page to respond to these – a) it's polite to reply to comments and b) you need to watch out for spam and complaints, and address them accordingly.

Stopping spam and dealing with complaints

Facebook is the main place where you might get comments and spam that you can't control. People do like to complain in public, and your Facebook page can easily come under attack.

It is possible to delete comments that other people make. Just be aware that if you delete complaints, the complainer is liable to share the fact that you've done that – a bit of polite damage limitation on the page itself is often more appropriate.

If someone spams my page, for example, by just posting a link to their page, I usually reply politely the first time (especially if the link is vaguely relevant), in case they've made a mistake, otherwise they get deleted.

This section covers two common concerns for people with a business Facebook page:

How do I delete a post or comment that someone has put on my Facebook page?

How do I ban or block someone from commenting on my Facebook page?

In fact, the way to do the second leads on from the first … so let's look at how to delete a comment first. For screenshots, please see the free resource on the Libro blog.[2]

How do I delete a post?

Comments move around a bit on Facebook, but if you've enabled people to be able to comment, you can see their comments under the heading **Posts to Page**. To look at all of these posts in detail or delete some, click on the **arrow at the top right**.

To delete a post OR to block or ban the user, click on the **down arrow** at the top right of the individual comment. You will now be presented with three options:

Hide from Page will hide the post but not delete it – no one will be able to see it. This would be useful if you suspected someone of posting inappropriately but wanted to get in touch with them to check what they meant or give them another chance / ask them to edit their post. You also have the option to ban the user at this point (use **Undo** to backtrack from here, the x button to hide and close the dialogue box, or **Ban User** to ban the user from the page).

---

[2] http://libroediting.com/2014/10/13/how-do-i-delete-a-post-or-ban-a-user-on-a-facebook-page/

Delete from Page will delete the post and give you the option to ban the person who wrote the post. You can **Delete the post and ban the user**, **Cancel** if you clicked this option by mistake, or just **Delete the post**. (You could use this option if the user had made a mistake, or posted something you didn't want on the page, but you don't actually want to ban that person from posting on your page in future.)

Embed Post will generate some HTML code that will allow you to include an image of the post on Facebook in other places such as your website or blog – useful if you have a great post from a fan or celebrity. Copy the code that's highlighted and use it anywhere that you can place HTML – in a blog post, on a website, in a discussion forum, etc.

How do I block someone from posting on my business's Facebook page?

As we've seen above, you can use two methods: both need you to look at the post itself first. You can then:

Hide the post and ban the user

Delete the post and ban the user

How do I stop people posting on my Facebook page at all?

If you want to suppress all posts from people who are not the Facebook page's administrators / moderators, go to **Settings / General / Posting Ability**. When you go to the **General area**, under **Posting Ability** you will see your current settings. If you want to change these, click **Edit**. This will allow you to choose whether and what people can post on your business page.

Use the **round buttons** to choose whether you **Allow other people to post to my Page timeline** or **Disable posts by other people on my Page timeline**. The tick boxes allow you to choose whether to let people add videos or photos (useful to untick if people have been posting inappropriate photos but you still want to allow comments) and allow you to ask Facebook to send you posts by other people that you then have to approve (you'll receive an email alerting you to the new post and allowing you to approve or reject it).

Click **Save Changes** to save your changes or **Cancel** if you want to keep your settings as they are.

Important notes about allowing posting and deleting post**s**

I personally think it's a good idea to allow other people to post on your business Facebook page.

After all, you want to encourage interaction and conversations, not just pump out sales information, right? I get a bit frustrated if I go onto the Facebook page for a business and find I can't place a comment about how much I loved their veggie sausages or enjoy wearing my new shoes. So, unless you are bombarded with spam and abuse, try not to use the Disable posts by other people on my timeline option if it all possible.

And a word on deleting posts. Be careful what you delete.

Posts it's OK to delete or hide

It's OK to delete or hide:

Unfounded or personal abuse

Spam that has nothing to do with your own page

Spam from rival companies in your business area who are not supporting and cooperating with you, but merely trying to get your followers to move over to them instead (for example, on my own editing page, posts from student proofreading companies just saying "For the best proofreading click here")

Pornographic or other inappropriate images, text or video

Posts it's best not to delete or hide

It's best not to delete or hide:

Genuine complaints and negative feedback – OK, so your first reaction will be to hide that post where someone complains the shoe they bought from your range has fallen apart. But if they've taken the time to find your Facebook page and complain, then they're going to know they did that, and they're going to notice if you delete it. What will they do then? At very least, post it again. But be assured that they will have told their friends and family, shared your page on their Facebook timeline with a note about what you've done, and been very unhappy altogether.

If someone posts a complaint or negative feedback on your Facebook page

What should you do if something negative does get on there? Consider these thoughts:

Think what you'd do if you encountered them in person. You wouldn't stick a bit of tape over their mouth or turn your back on them, would you? Yet that's what you're doing when you hide or delete their post.

Address the issue at least partly in public – for example, you could post a reply along the lines of, "Sorry to read you're experiencing problems. Please contact me at vvv@vvvvv.com or via my Contact Page [with link] so we can resolve your problem".

You could go further and say something like, "I'm sorry you appear to be having a problem – you can of course return your shoes to us for a full refund" and give them information on how to do this.

Once the problem is resolved, pop another reply on – "I'm glad we were able to replace your shoes and hope you're happy with the new pair – do let us know how you're getting on."

Be polite. If someone posts a little aggressively – "I've heard you supply slip-on shoes with fancy chains and blood diamonds on them to arms dealers: what do you say about that?" – then take the polite route, and address their question in public as far as you can.

Don't get into a fight in public – if it gets messy, take it offline with an offer to call them or whatever's appropriate.

If the poster strays into the inappropriate, follow the steps above for deleting or hiding posts, but maybe consider putting a note on the page to explain (calmly) why you did this.

This section has hopefully helped you to deal with negative or inappropriate comments and commentators on your Facebook page. You now know how to hide or delete comments and block or ban users from your Facebook business page, and how to use the Settings to control who can post what.

The golden rule of Facebook business pages

There's a golden rule that applies to all social media and that's Be Yourself. Allow your own personal self to appear on those pages. Have a picture of you on the profile, and comment and respond as appropriate.

It's also worth noting that your friends do not want to feel spammed by your business. I share my business page posts no more than once onto my personal timeline. I don't leap in to every personal conversation with, "Oh, I can proofread that," or, "Need some transcription? Just call me." It isn't appropriate, none of us like having that done to us, and it's a good way to annoy the very people who might otherwise be spreading the word about your business. By all means, mix business with pleasure, but make your business page pleasurable to read and keep your personal page personal as well as business-like.

Reciprocity on Facebook

This applies mainly to people using Facebook for their business, however it helps keep the wheels of general social interaction running smoothly, too!

If someone asks a question on your business page or a business-related question on your own timeline, always respond: my business page doesn't always alert me when I have a new comment – so keep checking yours to make sure you're not ignoring someone!

If someone sends you a Facebook message, always respond if it's appropriate and meant for you, not spam

Check your **Other messages** for messages from people who are not Friends but are making genuine contact, and respond appropriately

If people comment on your status updates, Like their comments and engage with them

If people share your status updates, Like the share and say thank you publicly or privately

If people recommend you via Facebook, thank the recommender and contact the prospect as soon as you can

Share other people's content

Like business pages as yourself and as your business (click on the cog next to Message)

If you join groups of peers, people in the same business, people who are also self-employed, etc., join in with the group once you're there, help other people and don't either relentlessly self-promote or stay silent

Facebook works on friendship and commonality. Share your peers' posts and you'll build up a network of people who will recommend, help and support you.

ALL ABOUT TWITTER

Using Twitter for your business

Twitter is an absolutely brilliant tool for business owners – if you use it in the right way. If you use in the wrong way, it can be a nightmare, as bad (or embarrassing) news travels very fast in the Twitter universe!

I personally got a lot out of Twitter in the early days, actually securing clients through using it – and long-term clients who recommended me on to more clients, too. It's been a major source of work for me, along with repeat business, personal recommendations and a specialist directory website. My clients still recommend me to other clients via Twitter, even several years on. (A music journalist once tweeted that she was looking for a transcriber. FIVE of my current clients tweeted her with my name!)

Benefits of Twitter: it's quick and easy to use. Disadvantage: it can be a time-sink. Most important thing to remember: people only tend to see a snapshot of their tweets every day – I only know one person who reads ALL of the tweets in his timeline. This means that your tweeting strategy should be a bit different from your other social media posting strategies.

Setting up your Twitter profile

When you join Twitter at www.twitter.com, it's very easy to set up a profile. Your profile is a quick guide to who you are. Anyone clicking on it or searching for it needs to know that they've found the right Liz Broomfield / Libro (or whatever) and to see easily what you do.

I and industry experts would recommend including the following:

Your real name when you log in, so that it shows on your tweets, keeping your company name for your Twitter ID

Your photograph on your profile, rather than your company logo (you can add that to your background)

Your company URL in the website field

Use your 140 letters of profile to the max, including what you do and any extra URLs

As with any profile, you can change or update it at any time; just click on your image in the top margin then **Settings** and choose **Edit Profile**, or if you're viewing your profile, click the **Edit Profile button**.

Following and followers

Once you've set up your Twitter account, you can start following a few people. Twitter will suggest ones that you don't really want, based on who's popular, but you can find interesting people to follow in a variety of ways. Obviously, the first is to look for people you know:

Ask someone for their Twitter ID when you meet them or glean it from their business card or website. Then enter that ID in the search field on Twitter

Or you can search for the person's name or company name in the **search field** on Twitter

Or you can go to http://www.twitter.com/ and add their Twitter ID (without an @ sign) after the slash

Have a look at their profile to check it's the correct person, then press the **Follow button** if it is.

If you're following someone in an interesting field, have a look at who they're following. If you click on their profile, you will see links to T**weets, Following** and **Followers**. Click on **Following** and have a look – there will be a handy **Follow button** by each name so you can simply follow from there (if you're already following someone, it will be marked as such).

Once you're viewing who someone is following, you will see a dropdown button marked **More** which will take you to their **Lists**. See more about **Lists** later on, but you can follow either an entire list or the members of one by clicking on the list, and this is another good way to glean people to follow in a particular area of interest.

How do I choose who to follow?

It's entirely up to you how many people you follow and whether you organise them in any way. When I'm deciding whether to follow people who I've found, or who have followed me (you don't HAVE to follow everyone who's followed you, but it's polite to at least have a look at their profile), this is what I do:

Check their profile to see whether they're interesting to me

Check their list of tweets to see if they tweet interesting information

Check their tweets for the same tweet repeated over and over again – this means a lack of imagination, something akin to spamming or an automated response

Check their tweets for regularity and date of tweeting – if someone tweets once a week or hasn't tweeted for a number of months, unless they're hugely important to me, I won't bother to follow them because their tweets will get lost in the general melee

I do also regularly run a check over the people I'm following (click on Home, your own Twitter ID and Following) to make sure they're still active. If not, I tend to cull. Sorry!

Lists

Lists are a great way to put the people who you follow into categories or filters that you can look at independently. For example, I have a "Must know" list which includes all of my real-life friends plus some news feeds that I follow, so that if I only have time for a quick dip into Twitter, I can see what's really important. I also have a "Journos" one so that I can see what my music journalist clients and a few others are up to, for some entertainment.

To add someone to a list:

Click on **their name** in your timeline to view their profile or go to your list of accounts followed (In your profile or on your home screen – **Following**)

Click the **User Options button** (next to **Following**, it looks like a cog)

Click on Add or Remove From Lists

You'll see a list of all of the lists you've already set up (if you have set any up) plus a button, **Create a List**

Either click on a list name to add that person then press the **X** in the top right corner to close the dialogue box or click on **Create a List** and make up a new list name to add this person to. (If you make a list private, only you can see it – you'll know when a list is private because it will have a padlock symbol next to the list name). Once you hit **Save list**, you will need to tick the particular list you want to add this person to.

Once you have some lists, you'll see a **Lists entry** on your profile. Ideas for lists include friends, particular interests, your business sector, news feeds, sport – anything you want.

You can follow other people's lists or mine them for good accounts to follow – just click on a particular person's Twitter ID and you'll see their following, followers and lists in the bar beneath their cover picture. It's also worth playing with the **Discover** feature, although only once you're following a few 'real' people, otherwise you'll just be offered celebrities.

Note – these instructions are for the basic web-based Twitter interface. It doesn't work in exactly the same way on mobile devices or third-party Twitter management dashboards.

How Twitter works – @ and

Two things that you'll see a lot of on Twitter are the symbols @ and #

@ is used in front of a Twitter ID to notify the person that you're talking to them or to point someone else to their account. For example, someone might recommend an account for me to follow:

Megmac: @lyzzybee_libro have a look at @thecreativepenn for a good feed for writers

This makes the message appear in my **Notifications list** (see below) and TheCreativePenn's Notifications list, so I will see the recommendation and she will see that she's been recommended to me. If she wants, she can then reach out to me, and say thank you to the recommender. (Note, if you want a recommendation to be public, you need to put something before the first @, such as a full stop or another word: "Hey, @lyzzybee_libro have a look at …"

is used to create clickable links that will pull information on a particular topic together in one view. It's often used at events and conferences – so, for example, #cbsms is used by people tweeting about the Central Birmingham Social Media Surgery. When you see a hashtag (as this is called) in a tweet, it will be a clickable link. Click on the hashtag and you will see all of the recent tweets

with that hashtag, giving you a view of what's going on and who's talking about it.

Lyzzybee_libro: Off to the social media surgery to help a few people today #cbsms

It is also used to link tweets on a wider topic, e.g. #amwriting, which writers use to talk about the writing process. You can pop a hashtag on a tweet when you want it to come up in such searches; for example I might tweet about my book on transcription and add #transcription at the end, so that anyone looking at that hashtag will see my tweet.

Your Twitterstream and mentions

Whether you're viewing Twitter online on a computer or via a phone or a third party dashboard, you will have a Twitterstream and then various other views:

Home will show you your Twitterstream: all the most recent tweets by people / companies / whatever that you're following.

Your **Notifications list** will show you anything directly concerning your own Twitter account – so messages that mention you with an @[your Twitter ID] as well as people who have followed you. It's good practice to keep an eye on this so that you can reply to any messages sent to you and say thank you for recommendations and follows. Note here that

Notifications gives you information on who's followed you and favourited your messages, and any messages that start with or include your name.

Getting rid of spammers

Everyone gets spammed by Twitter accounts, dodgy or otherwise, that are usually either looking for random followers to boost their numbers or clicks to their undesirable links. The ones with links often only have a link in the text – this is a real red flag and you should never click on a link in a tweet, even from a friend, if there's only a link and no text (your friend could have had their account hacked).

If you receive an odd tweet or one with just a link, click on the photo or name of the sender. You will typically see that they've sent the same short message, or no message and just a link, to multiple people. Click on the **User Actions button** on their profile and you have options to **Block** or **Report**.

Once you've clicked on **Block** or **Report** you will get the chance to explain why exactly you are blocking or reporting the person. This alerts Twitter that the person is spamming, and will help to save someone not as savvy as you from clicking on a dodgy link and going who knows where in cyberspace!

If you're just getting annoyed or bored by a Twitter account that you follow, you can click on their photo or name and press the button marked

Following – this will change to **Unfollow** as you hover over it; click it and you'll unfollow them and no longer see them in your Twitterstream.

You can find screenshots for all of this information on the Libro blog.[3]

Golden rules for using Twitter effectively

Using Twitter effectively is a matter of knowing how it works and how people view it, and being sensible and polite.

Posting multiple times

The main point about tweeting is that very few people read every single tweet on their timeline. People typically check Twitter on the way to work, at lunchtime, on the way home, and at some time in the evening. Once you're following more than about fifty people, there's no way that you're going to see all of their tweets – so think of people as viewing a snapshot of their Twitterstream rather than everything.

This means that it's fine to tweet a message multiple times, where it would be seen as rude and

---

[3] http://libroediting.com/2014/07/16/using-twitter-for-your-business/

intrusive to post a Facebook status multiple times in one day.

You also need to be aware of your markets and their time zones – if you have a lot of Australian clients, and you're in the UK, you will need to tailor your tweets to their time zone, maybe investing in a Twitter dashboard that will allow you to pre-schedule your tweets.

Using a dashboard

It can be very useful to use a dashboard such as Tweetdeck to manage your Twitter accounts. You can view and post from multiple accounts at a time (handy if you have, say, a personal and a work account) and view your lists in their own feeds. Some of them will also allow you to schedule your tweets to be published at a certain time or on a certain date, which can be very useful (although make sure that you still keep an eye on when these go out, as there have been numerous examples of a tweet auto-posting when it's really not appropriate, such as after a disaster).

Sharing other people's material

The other main rule is to be polite and reciprocate and say thank you.

If you retweet other people's tweets, they are more likely to share your tweets with their network. To retweet, click on the word retweet underneath the tweet, or look for that 'arrows-in-a-square' icon which has the same effect. Some people reckon that you should share four other tweets to every one of your own that you post. I'm not that scientific, but I do try to share as much as I post.

Saying thank you and being proactive

If other people retweet or otherwise share your tweets (which you will find out about by reviewing your Notifications feed) do drop them a message to say thank you.

If someone recommends your Twitter account or your services to someone else, contact the person to whom you're being recommended with a polite "how can I help you" and a way to contact you, and say thank you to the recommender.

Not automating too much and not spamming

I'm not a big fan of the automated message when I follow someone's Twitter account, and many other people find this annoying, too. I like to know that there's a person behind the account. Similarly, all sales and no sharing, or all automated tweeting and no replying to @ messages will probably get people irritated.

Searching for jobs on Twitter

Here's a worked example of how to search for jobs on Twitter. You can find all the screenshots and a full worked example on the Libro blog.[4]

Why search for jobs on Twitter?

People talk a LOT on Twitter, and they also use it for information seeking purposes. How many times have you seen a friend, or just someone you follow, ask a question or look for a recommendation? People will throw a question out: "Does anyone know a good transcriber?" and other people will answer them. If you're a freelancer, it's brilliant if one of your own clients does this and gives your name (this happens quite regularly to me, so I promise it happens), but if not, as long as you're not over pushy about it, there is no harm in tweeting to that person to tell them about your services.

Does searching for jobs on Twitter really work?

Yes. Yes it does. I can say that with certainty, because I know it does from experience. Here are just a couple of examples:

-----

[4]http://libroediting.com/2013/12/23/searching-for-jobs-on-twitter/

I ran my regular search (see below for how to do this) on "looking for proofreader". I found a Tweet by a woman working in PR. I contacted her, she became a client, she took me with her when she joined a big agency, and when she left that agency, I ended up with them and her as clients.

A journalist I followed on Twitter posted the tweet "Can anyone help me with some transcription?" At the time, I didn't offer transcription as a service, but I was a trained audio-typist. I got in touch. Again, it went to email for the negotiations, and I ended up with that journalist as a long-term client. Plus, she recommended me (via Twitter and email) to other people, who also recommended me, and I ended up with a client base of music journalists.

So yes, it does work. Here's how to do it.

First, make sure your profile represents you accurately

When you tweet to someone, the first thing they're going to do is look at your profile. So make sure it includes all of the details we discussed in the previous section.

How do I search in Twitter?

At the top of the screen, you will find a **grey box with a magnifying glass icon** in the right-hand end. You can type any words you want to search for in here and hit **Return** to run your search.

You do need to think about your search terms and what you think people who might be searching for your expertise might need. For example, a cookery book proofreader might use "writing cookery book", on the grounds that if someone is writing one, they are going to need editing help at some stage. Input your term, hit **Return**, and when the results come up, choose **All** rather than **Top** or **People you follow** – to make the results list as wide as possible.

How do I interpret the Twitter search results?

Bear in mind what you're looking for: people who might need your help. Scan down the results list, and you'll soon see some hopeful ones. The cookery book proofreader could send a quick note to all of the people who are talking about writing a cookery book, but not reply to tweets which just mention a cookery book, and are not really associated with someone writing one right now.

Advanced search in Twitter

Twitter searching doesn't use wild cards, which means you can't input something like cook* book and get it to search for cookery book, cook book, cooking book, etc. Once upon a time, you'd have to run searches for all the different words you wanted. But now you can run Advanced Search and search for lots of different things at the same time.

Once you've got your first search results, you will see an option for **Advanced search in the left-hand sidebar**. Pick **Advanced search** and you'll be taken to the Advanced Search input screen. Here you can handily choose words that must be included in the results, and words that could be included. So, our proofreader could ask that all tweets that Twitter finds must include the words "writing book", but they can also include any of "cooking", "cookery", "cook" and "recipe". This means that it will look for "writing book" plus any one or more of the other words.

What effect does this have on the results? Give it a go and you'll soon find you get more results doing this than for each of lots of different individual searches, all in one place.

How do I save a Twitter search?

When you've found a good search that has a lot of useful results (no search will have ALL useful results), you can save the search. Just choose **Save from the top right of your search results screen.** When you next click in the search field, you will get a list of **Recent searches** and **Saved searches**. Your current search is in **Recent searches**, but will stay in **Saved searches** once you've saved it. This means that you can just click on that search query rather than typing it all in again.

How often should I re-run my Twitter job searches?

I recommend running each of your searches every 24 hours. This gives you only a few extra results each time, it's easy to note where the ones that you've already seen start, and if you want to reply to a tweet, it's not too long since the person tweeted it.

It might be worth running them more frequently at first, but keep an eye on how many new results come up during 24 hours and you'll get an idea of the schedule to use. I wouldn't leave it longer than 24 hours, for fear of missing out, as Twitter is a very immediate medium.

How do I pitch for a job on Twitter?

You might feel a bit uneasy about this. But I can promise you that no one minds one short, friendly and non-pushy contact in reply to a tweet they've sent out. I've sent loads, I've had a certain amount of success; some people have ignored me, but no one has ever complained.

This is how I'd approach this situation as a proofreader looking for work on cookery books:

@Writing_cookbook Do you need an editor for your cookbook? If so, maybe you'd like to talk. Do drop me a line if interested. Thanks!

So, a very non-pushy, friendly and polite tweet inviting them to respond. If they did respond positively, I'd very quickly move to giving them my website URL (even though it's on my profile, I'd put it in a tweet) and initiate email contact so we could discuss the project in more detail.

So there we go: that's how I searched for jobs on Twitter – and won them. I haven't actively used Twitter for job searching for a while now (as I have a full schedule), but you know what? I still have both of those original clients who I talked about above! And I'm still active on Twitter, sharing other people's content with my followers if I think it will interest them and help the other person.

Reciprocity on Twitter

Here are some top tips on how to reciprocate on Twitter to optimise the great opportunities it can bring:

Always respond to @ comments that require a reply (i.e. they ask you a question or tell you about something)

Always respond to RTs, Follow Friday mentions, etc., with a thank you Tweet

If someone recommends you to someone else, always a) thank the original person, b) make contact with the prospect – don't wait for them to come to you

Take part in peer-group events like #watercoolermoment etc. to encourage the people who run them and engage with your peers – you are likely to find new, interesting people to follow and talk to

Retweet other people's content if it is interesting to you / your followers. People often talk about the 80/20 rule – 8 retweets or shares of other people's content via the social media sharing buttons on their blog posts to 2 promoting your own words or interests

Remember: Twitter works fast. Many people don't see their whole stream, just snapshots through the day. If someone has seen your content and contacted you / shared, etc., try to thank them within 12 hours or less.

Use Twitter to forge links, have short conversations, support and encourage others and share content with your followers. People who you retweet will be more likely to retweet your posts. People who you recommend to others will remember the favour.

ALL ABOUT LINKEDIN

Using LinkedIn for your business

LinkedIn is seen primarily as a networking tool for the more corporate end of the market. However, you can set up your own business page on LinkedIn now, and there is a lot more interactivity and 'social' activity than there used to be – or than you might think.

Setting up a LinkedIn profile

You can join LinkedIn and set up your profile at www.linkedin.com.

It's a good idea to include as much information as you can on here – and in a professional way. While it's never a good idea to allow typos and grammatical errors on any profile, it's vitally important here, as people tend to make more of an effort, and so any errors will be particularly glaring.

There are various sections to fill in on the profile. Including past jobs allows your 'network' to grow, as LinkedIn, unlike other social media, will not let you even request to connect to just anyone. For example, I've added all of my main jobs to **Experience**, and I've added information about the books I've written in the **Publications** section.

Finding your way around LinkedIn

Your home page will contain a feed a little like your Facebook timeline, with updates from people to whom you're linked. To find people to link to, you can search in the search box at the top of the screen. Once you're linked to someone, they will appear in your Connections list, which you can access by clicking the [number] connections icon where you see it.

You can see your **Invitations** and **Notifications** at the top right. **Invitations** allow you to see who has invited you to connect and any messages they've sent you via LinkedIn. **Notifications** show you who has liked your updates or shared your profile.

Linking to people on LinkedIn

LinkedIn is different from other social media networks, in that you have to have a tangible connection to a person in order to "Link" to them. If you find someone you want to link to and press **Connect**, you'll be asked how you know that person. If you say that they're a colleague, or that you've done business with them, you'll be asked which of your jobs they are a colleague from – that's why it's important to list all of the companies that you have worked for on your profile. If you say that they're a friend, you'll be asked to prove you know them by providing their email address.

You can find people just outside your network by clicking on the **People You May Know** link. This will give you a list of either friends of friends or people who have said that they work or have worked at the same organisations that you've worked at. You can connect to these people in the same way. You can also search for people using the search box at the top of the screen.

However you access them, click on the person's name to see their profile and then use the Connect button to ask them to link to you. LinkedIn will then ask you how you know that person: when you click on one of the radio buttons, you will be asked for more detail.

Setting up a company page

You can set up a company page on LinkedIn for your business – this will give people another way to find you and will provide another link to your website and other social media.

To set up a company page, click on **Interests** at the top, then **Companies** from the drop-down. At the top right of the next page you'll find a link for **Add Company**.

You will first need to confirm that you're eligible to create and moderate this page, so there will be an email sent to you to confirm that you are indeed eligible, and you must have a personal LinkedIn account to create a company page.

Fill in all of your company's details and save – and there you go. To edit your company information, find the company page and click on **Edit**.

Getting social

This section is about social media – so how do you get social on LinkedIn?

Updates

You can post updates, just like on Facebook – do this from the Home page. Your updates will appear on your connections' home pages, just as theirs do on yours. You can like and share updates in a very similar way to Facebook.

You can direct most blogging platforms to automatically post links on LinkedIn – all of my WordPress blog posts do this.

You can also link your Twitter account to LinkedIn by going to your **account settings** (click on the small photo in the top right of the screen), clicking on your name and choosing **Manage Twitter Accounts**. Click on **Add your Twitter account**. If you're logged in to Twitter you will see an **Authorize app** message, if you're not logged in, you will be asked to log in first.

Recommendations and Endorsements

If someone has done a good job for you, you can click on **Recommend** in their profile and type in a recommendation. They will be emailed this and will have the option as to whether to publish it or not (this prevents people posting negative comments without the member knowing).

You can also **Endorse** people, choosing a skill that you know they have and clicking to confirm you agree they have it, or even adding a new one to their list.

Groups

There are thousands of interest groups on LinkedIn and these can be a good way to meet new people, spread the word about what you're doing, and find out what other people are up to.

Access **Groups** by searching in the top search bar (you can click on the icon to the left of the search area and select only **Groups** to search) or by clicking on **Interests** then **Group**s. Once you've joined some Groups, you will find them listed on your Groups page, and then some suggestions underneath.

Groups work very simply – you can post a new message or reply to another one, just as in other social media like Facebook and Google+. You can choose whether you are updated by email for all posts and replies in the group, or whether you want to just access them via the LinkedIn website.

I have found that some groups do become clogged with too many adverts and not enough discussion, but others can be really useful. The usual rules apply about reciprocity and kindness when using LinkedIn for social media communications.

You can find screenshots for these instructions on the Libro blog.[5]

Golden rules for using LinkedIn

Be professional. LinkedIn is known as a professional and careers-orientated site, although there is certainly room for the self-employed. But you do need to be extra-professional and not very personal on here.

Reciprocate. If people like and share your updates and group posts, say thank you and like and share theirs.

Similarly, if people recommend or endorse you, do try to recommend and endorse them back.

---

[5]http://libroediting.com/2014/04/09/using-linkedin-for-your-business/

Reciprocity on LinkedIn

Reciprocity on LinkedIn is just like it is for any other site, but there are some specifics, too:

When you link to someone, change the standard message to a personal one, maybe reminding them where you met or making another tailored comment: some people get quite annoyed with the standard messages and might even ignore then on principle, so it's worth making that extra effort

Introduce people who you think would be useful to each other

Press that **Endorse** button and give your contact some more stats

Use the **Recommend** feature if you've worked with someone to place some feedback on their profile; LinkedIn displays how many recommendations you've made, and everyone wants to work with someone who's generous with feedback and honest praise

If someone endorses or recommends you, or introduces you to a third party, send them a message to say thank you

Join groups and share content kindly and generously

When you join a group, get to know people and comment on other posts and questions before you start self-promoting

If a group seems to be full of spam and self-promotion and no discussion and mutual encouragement, leave it alone – you won't be able to change it and it'll just annoy you – but learn from that what not to do!

LinkedIn can be a very powerful tool for IT and other business people, with most recruiters looking for a LinkedIn profile these days. Make sure that your full CV is on there, and a good photo.

ALL ABOUT GOOGLE+

Using Google+ for your business

Because I don't want to show my home address in public on Google, or give it to Google, most of the examples here are drawn from setting up a **Brand**. However, the principles are the same if you're setting up a local business with an address. Access all of the screenshots and full instructions here.

Why should I set up a Google+ account and page?

This is a good question, as Google+ is known to be one of the rather less active social media platforms, although there are active communities in Google+ and Hangouts and other social discussions and groupings. However, the clue is in the word "Google". Basically, stuff you post on Google+ and your Google+ page will be indexed more quickly by Google and will appear as more relevant in a Google search. I auto-post to Google+ from my blogs, but even this minimal effort is worth making for the indexing and the effect it has on search results.

How do I set up a Google+ account?

If you have a Google email address, you will automatically have a Google+ account. Look at the top of your email and you'll see a +[your name] icon. You do need to have a Google account to have a Google+ account, although of course you don't need to use it for anything else. Notifications about Google+ interactions come to your Gmail, but you could set up an autoforward to send that to another email account. Anyway, click on the +[name] icon and you'll be taken to your Google+ account.

Once you're in Google+, you'll find that it looks quite a lot like other social media platforms such as Facebook, with posts by friends, recommended contacts and a place to post an update at the top. We're not going to explore personal G+ here, but instead look at the business application.

How do I set up a Google+ page for my business?

To access the Google+ pages creator and editor, click on the **Home button** at top left and choose **Pages**. This will lead you to an option to choose a business type.

Clicking on **Storefront** or **Service Area** (which is what I chose when I first did this) will first give you an option to search for a business. If you choose **Create New Page**, as you would expect to do, after clicking **Not a Local Business** you will get the option to add a business with a street address. This is great if you have a shop or trading address, for example if you welcome people into a high street shop, have a gym in an out-of-town location or have customers visit your home to collect products, have therapeutic sessions, etc. If this is the case, you can fill in all the details and have a listing for your business appear on Google Maps for prospective customers to see (if they search for your business name or just look at the map at a certain zoom level).

But what if I don't want to list my address and have a pin on Google Maps?

I don't want to list my address on Google Maps because I work from home, but I don't see any clients here and I don't really want the world to know my address! So this is how to set up a Google+ page without your address. Note, you can't cheat the section above and put in spaces or dots – it really does want to pinpoint your address with a little label.

When you're at the point of choosing your business type, choose **Brand** if you don't want to have to add your address. This will take you to a screen where you start to add your details. You can add in your URL and select the type of thing you're talking about – so this is how you set up a community or other non-business entity, too.

Do note that you need to tick the box to agree to the **Pages Terms** (and do click through to have a look and check you DO agree) and to confirm that you're authorised to create the page. Then click **Create Page**.

Once you've created your page, Google+ will give you a tour or you can just start customising your page. This is all pretty self-explanatory. For example, you will be asked to complete your profile and given options to share updates. There's also a section where you can see Insights – how people are interacting with your new page.

You can add your own cover image and picture to appear on the left of the banner at the top of the page. Once you've clicked **Change cover** or **Change profile picture**, you can choose one from the gallery or upload your own photo (if you have already put up several cover photos, you can click on that link to choose one you've used earlier).

Once you've added the pictures, you can explore and add updates, contact information and links.

How do I edit my Google+ business page(s)?

You can access your business pages at any time by clicking the **Home button** and choosing **Pages**. If you've created more than one Page, you will be shown all the ones you have active, with a link to edit them.

You can find screenshots for these instructions on the Libro blog.[6]

---

[6] http://libroediting.com/2014/10/22/google-for-business/

The Golden Rules of Google+

The rules here are the same as everywhere on social media:

Be professional

Reciprocate and share

Reciprocity on Google+

Google+ works much like Facebook, in that you can +1 (Like) posts, make comments etc. The major point about Google+ is that if you share your content and others' on there, Google will pick up on it and add it to its search engine that little bit more quickly. So it is worth engaging on there even if it isn't as busy or active as the other networks.

OTHER SOCIAL MEDIA PLATFORMS

Reciprocity on Pinterest, Tumblr, etc.

Although I'm not going into detail about some of the more image-orientated social media platforms, they can be very useful for, for example, craft and arts businesses. The rules of reciprocity remain the same as on all of the other platforms:

Be kind

Share others' material before you expect them to share yours

Say thank you when people share your posts, images and shares

Respond to comments, good or bad

WEBSITES AND BLOGGING

A word about websites and blogging

Is it worth having a website for my business?

In my networking adventures and other travels in the world of small business, I come across quite a few people who don't have a website. To be honest, I'm a bit shocked when this happens. Unless you've got a reliable pool of clients, with new ones on the horizon to fill in gaps if you lose any, then you'll want to be findable.

When you think about getting the roof done, or finding a cleaner, or sourcing flowers for an event, or buying a product, where do you look?

Online.

Even if you look for a tradesperson on a Yellow Pages style website, I bet you like to have a URL to click through to, to look at their details. Right?

If you don't have a website, or even a single page with your name / company name and information about yourself, then what will people find when they search for you?

People come to my website in one of four ways:

- They search for my name
- They search for my company name
- They search for something that I do
- They search for the answer to a question ("is it en route or on route?" "How do I repeat the header row of a Word document on every page?")

This is what would happen if I didn't have a website:

- If they searched for my name, they'd find my Twitter or Facebook feed, or photos of me socially, or mention of me on forums – all fine, but they'd probably rather find either my business Facebook page or my company information in one place
- If they searched for my company name, they would find my Facebook or Twitter feed, however, these mention and feed back to my

website, as they're not enough in themselves to maintain interest and get me business
- If they searched for something that I do, they'd find someone else's website and if they were looking for someone to do that work, they'd hire that someone else
- If they searched for an answer to a question, someone else would answer it, and if they're looking for someone to work for them, they'd hire that someone else

This is what happens because I have a website:

- If they search for my name, they find my website and my other feeds, which all link together; they find out what I do and if they want to talk about work, they can contact me
- If they search for my company name, they find my website, find out what I do, and possibly hire me, getting in touch via my contact form
- If they search for something that I do, they find my website, find out that I do that, find references from people who I've done that for before, and possibly hire me – getting in touch via my contact form
- If they search for an answer to a question, if I can answer it, they find out that I know what I'm talking about, and note me for later or sign up to receive emails when I post, and might hire me in time, ask me a question or engage with my blog

What should be on my website?

The bare minimum

As a bare minimum, you should have a page somewhere that includes:

- Your name
- Your company name (if it's different)
- A list of your services or products – make sure that you mention all of the forms of the things you do on that page (so I would include transcriber, transcription services, editor, editing, etc.)
- References from satisfied customers
- A way to get in touch with you – a contact form, a phone number (most people like to see this), an email address
- Professionally produced text – by which I really mean have someone check it for typos and spelling mistakes which will seriously undermine your reputation and send people running from your services – whatever they are

It's a good idea to have your company name in the url for your website, but personally I don't hold it against small companies if they have the word "blogspot" or "wordpress" in their URL – you don't need to pay extra to have that if you don't want to.

You can use a Facebook page as your company web page, however I would hesitate to use ONLY something that changes so often as Facebook. A company Facebook page is better than nothing, however!

If you haven't got a website, and you haven't got a steady stream of new and regular customers giving you a good income stream, I really do suggest that you get a website!

Optional extras

You can add these extras if you want and if they add value. If you find that you're getting a steady stream of enquiries via your simple website, and they turn into paying customers, then only add these items if you can see a clear value in doing so, rather than doing it out of vanity or because someone's persuaded you to buy their service:

A URL that's just your company name – you will have to pay for this, probably renewing annually

A professionally designed website – there are many "themes" on offer that look as good as professional websites

A blog – this is GREAT for driving people to your website and setting you up as an expert in your field; if you only do one of these things, write a simple blog

Someone to write web text and blog posts for you

Search Engine Optimisation – a professional can ensure that you're showing up in search engines etc., but shop around – this can be expensive and there are lots of things you can do to SEO your site on your own (just have a little search engine search and see what you can find)

A shopping cart and catalogue – very useful if you're producing craft items or any tangibles – but you can sign up to services like Etsy and eBay which will do this for you

The big caveat

It's really important to have a web presence so that people can find you.

It's really important to be super-vigilant, because unscrupulous companies prey on small businesses' lack of expertise in this area:

Always ask around fellow small-business owners or someone whose website you admire and see who they use

If someone offers to make you top of the search engine results, ask what other sites they've worked on (always ask for references anyway) and do a search for yourself

If someone offers to revolutionise your website and make you a millionaire overnight, they're probably over-selling – ask for references

If someone offers to build your website make sure –
no, MAKE SURE – that you will be able to edit and
update the text and pictures on that website
whenever you want to. Never hand over the full
ownership of your site to another person such that
you can't update it yourself.

10 reasons to write a blog

Why should you write a blog? Why should you start
writing a blog, and why should you continue
writing a blog? Here are my top reasons why. I'm
really looking at business blogging here, but the
first one applies to everyone!

1. Because you want to

This reason covers both personal bloggers and
business bloggers. You should start writing, and
continue writing, a blog, because you want to.
Forcing yourself to do something you don't want to
do is no fun, and you should enjoy the time you
spend designing and honing your blog and writing
those entries. Whether you want to share holiday
pictures or reviews of restaurants or share your
professional expertise, do it because you want to.

2. You've got something interesting to talk about

There are so many interesting things to talk about. I
often meet people running businesses but I have no
idea of the nitty-gritty of their everyday lives. How

does a carpenter learn his trade? What does a freelance solicitor do, day-to-day? How many projects does a crafter have on the go at any one time, and how do mobile hairdressers help their clients to choose a new hairstyle?

I found that my posts on building my business struck a chord and interested many people. A few posts that I made, really for myself, about hints and tips for using Word has turned into a popular series. If you run a business, think about some of the behind the scenes things, some of the aspects of your knowledge that people might be interested to know about (don't worry about giving away your secrets – I might publish articles on Word headings and tables of contents, but I still get asked to do them by my clients!).

Of course, it goes without saying that you shouldn't share personal details about your clients. But I think it's fine to talk about them if they're heavily disguised – or ask if they'd like to have a case study published with links back to their website!

3. It will set you up as an expert in your field

This is invaluable when you're building your reputation and your business. Don't see it as giving away information for nothing, think of it as sharing your expertise with the world. Once you start appearing in people's Google searches when they're trying to resolve a problem, they'll be more likely to come to you for help when they need your services. If you can offer a back catalogue of useful, targeted advice on your blog when you're negotiating with a new prospect, they will see that you can walk the walk as well as talk the talk.

This may not lead directly to sales – but I've often seen my blog posts shared among other people and organisations in my field. Keep your name in front of them as well as prospects, and you never know where the next recommendation and job might come from!

4. It will attract people to your site

This links in to the above point. The more content there is on your website, and the more it is packed full of keywords and language to do with your business, the more findable it is in the search engines. The more people find information that is useful to them and engages them, the more time they will spend on your website. The more time people spend on your website, or the more repeat visits they make, or the fact that they're getting regular updates into their RSS* reader or email inbox, the more likely they are to remember your name and your products or services when they, or a contact, need them.

 *What's this RSS stuff? RSS feeds are file formats that allow your regularly updated content to be collected and sent on to people, usually in order to allow them to read all of the blogs etc. that interest them using an RSS reader that accumulates everything they want in one place. Examples of RSS readers include Feedly. RSS feeds can be found on blogs, often represented by a little orange square with white lines on it.

More website visitors does not directly lead to more sales in a quantifiable way. But as long as you show genuine expertise and a willingness to engage with your audience, you will build your exposure, get more visitors to your site, and this will help you to become better known and gain more sales.

5. It will build your platform

Your platform is the group of people who are engaged with you in whatever way – through personal connections, social media such as Twitter, Facebook and LinkedIn, through your email newsletter, through your blog – and who can then be "leveraged" (horrible word) when you want to get the word out about something new that you're offering.

For example, if you're self-publishing a book, it's vital to have built a circle of connections before it comes out, so you have a guaranteed audience of at least a few people. If you start offering a new service, for example when I added transcription services to my proofreading and editing offering, it's useful to have people who you can tell and who will then, hopefully, spread the word.

Having a blog builds your platform because it engages people's interest. It brings them to your website, it gets them reading your content regularly, and it encourages them to sign up for your RSS feed or to receive your posts by email as they're published. Once you have subscribers, you can get information out to that guaranteed audience when you need to. That's much harder if you only have a static website for them to visit.

6. Regularly updated content will boost your position in search engine search results

It's fairly common knowledge that the search engines (Google, Yahoo, etc.) like content that is regularly updated. This means that their complex and little-known (and ever-changing) algorithms will promote websites that are frequently updated above those that are static. Updating your blog once a week or more gives all of the content on your website a better chance of being found by potential contacts and clients, because it gives it a better chance of appearing in a higher position in the search results.

7. So will information crammed full of the keywords that are important in your industry

Keywords are vital for search engines, too. If you just write a set of keywords over and over again, the chances are the search engines will pick up that it's not real content, and will not show it to searchers.

But if you are writing well-crafted copy which includes a good sprinkling of keywords among the text, you will find yourself doing better in the search engine results.

I write natural text in my blog posts that are (hopefully) interesting and give something to the reader – but I am also careful to include relevant keywords at a regular rate, which improves my search engine optimisation (SEO) no end (it's also good to get them into sub-headings and the blog title itself). SEO is a fairly dark art, but the more keywords you can sensibly insert into your content, the more the search engines will be happy to find and display your content to their users.

8. You want to engage with your readers / prospects / clients

Blogs are not a one-way conversation. Once your audience has built a bit, you will get comments, shares, etc. on your blog posts, and on the places where you promote them (I will get almost as many comments on my Facebook post advertising a new blog post as I will on the post itself).

One of the golden rules of blogging is that you need to respond to your comments. Some bloggers are very good at this, some are not. I'm sure everyone's commented excitedly on a blog post, only to find their comment is effectively "ignored", with no reply from the writer. I think that's quite rude, and I am likely to engage a lot less – or stop engaging –

with bloggers who have a habit of not replying. Obviously, we all get times when we're away or too busy to reply that moment, but most blogging platforms alert users to replies, and you want to keep that feature switched on and engage with your audience, otherwise they will stop coming back.

And those commenters might just be your friend Ali or your ex-colleague Steph, but every person who engages with your blog is a potential client or recommender.

9. You want to engage with other bloggers

There's nothing like blogging for building communities of like-minded people. Once you're blogging in a niche area, whether it be fiction writing, editing, ironing services or Sage, people who are interested in the same sorts of areas will start to follow your blog, comment on your posts and share what you're saying.

This is useful for a couple of reasons: firstly, it's always good to have colleagues. I've written elsewhere about how I treat other people in the same line of business as me as colleagues rather than competitors. It's always good to have people to recommend prospects on too if you're fully booked and can't take them on, and to have people to send you referrals. Sometimes you need to have a moan or a chat or ask advice, and you might want to do this privately rather than publicly, which is where your network of colleagues can come in very handy.

You can also read what they're saying, get new ideas, keep up to date, and slot into networks that offer mutually useful posts, services and applications.

Secondly, this may give you the opportunity to guest post on other people's blogs, and vice versa. We'll talk about sharing your content in other places next. If I hadn't started blogging, I wouldn't have got to know many of the editors I now know who link to my blog articles, share them on social media, and act as a sounding-board when I need to talk things through. That's worth every hour of effort I put into my blog, to be honest!

10. You want to share your content in other places on the web

The good thing about your URLs and name appearing in places on the web that are not connected directly with you, your website and social media pages is – you guessed it – it boosts your position in search engine results. The more times your URL appears on a website that's on a solid standing itself and has followers and people talking about it, the more the search engines will consider your website to be appropriate to present in their search results listings.

These links to your content on other people's pages are called backlinks. You can secure these in a number of ways:

Comment on someone else's blog post and include your URL
Contribute when someone asks for examples, experiences or feedback, again making sure that your URL is included
Write a guest blog post for someone – ensuring that the biography at the end includes all of your links

If you've ever allowed comments on a website or blog you'll know that a lot of companies do this seemingly randomly, just to get their URL into other people's comments, and now you know why they do it. So do make sure that the content and comments you share are appropriate to the topic of the post on which you're commenting! But this is a great way to increase traffic to your website and blog.

Reciprocity on blogs

I'm including blogs in social media because blogs that work best for businesses and people who want a "successful" blog are those whose owners engage in two-way conversation, share content and link people together. Sounds like social media to me!

On your own blog, mention and link to people who have helped, advised or inspired you

ALWAYS reply to comments. If you don't have time to reply to each individually, at least put up a thank you and a mention to the most important ones

Keep an eye on your search statistics and respond to what your readers are looking for (e.g. I noticed people were searching for "comment boxes too large" so added new blog post about that)

If people like and comment on your blog, pop over to their blog and scatter a few comments and likes if you find their content interesting

Use those social media buttons on other people's blogs to share their content – and make sure you enable the ones on your blog to allow and encourage people to share

Engage with other bloggers especially in your industry sector or area of interest – comment, share, etc.

Offer guest post spots on your blog for other people to contribute content

If you give someone a guest blog spot, make sure that you include all their links as well as a little biography about them – make it easy for people to find them.

If you place a guest post on someone else's blog, make sure that you give them all of your links to include, and talk about it as much as possible on your other social media channels

Blogs can be a powerful way to meet people, link with people, learn from people and get your content shared around the world.

HOW TO MAINTAIN A GOOD ONLINE REPUTATION

You are your brand. I know that that sounds a bit marketing-speaky, but it's true. If you run a business, people are going to look for you yourself online as well as your business name. I can vouch for that, because I get loads of searches coming through to my blog for the people I feature in my Small Business Chat interviews. Far more of them are looking for the person's name than for their business name (if it's different). Here are the methods that I use for maintaining a good and positive online image, with some tips which should be useful for you, too.

These tips mostly relate to social media, but you can extend them to anywhere where people see you, and your business, in operation, such as networking events, trade fairs, etc.

What do you mean by "You are your brand"?

This is particularly important if you run a small business or are a sole trader. However, even if you look at a multinational, the person at the head of the company and their personal reputation has an effect on the perception of the company.

Think about Richard Branson. What about Theo Paphitis and Duncan Bannatyne? Remember Gerald Ratner and how he ruined his business with one sentence, announcing in public that his company's products were "crap"?

In the same way, when you go out networking, or you do stuff online, and you run a business, people are getting an impression of you which extends to the perception they have of your business.

My personal dos and don'ts

This is of course a personal list. I know that I'm ultra-careful about my brand and company reputation, but I'd rather be ultra-careful than too relaxed. Reputations can be destroyed in an instant!

This is not about manipulating your image to sell more of your product or service; it's about making sure that you're representing your company in a positive light and making sure you match in your behaviour the message that you want your business to get across.

DO be yourself

It's no good trying to hide who you are. Yes, if you're shy, you can project more of an image of self-assurance, but also kindness, respect and care often come with shyness, and they're good things for your clients to see. Personally, I'm very open and honest, and I try to give something back through charity donations and helping people. Therefore I have made microbusiness loans to celebrate Libro's anniversary, and help out other small businesses with weekly features where I interview a small-business owner and give them some publicity, etc. I also keep my blog posts linked to what I do and my own practice – someone mentioned to me just the other day that my posts are very personal and friendly, which is how I hope my business comes across, too.

DO stay true to your morals and ideals

I also try to make sure that what I do with Libro mirrors my own personal morals and ideas. This is why I won't put ads on my blogs unless it's a testimonial for someone's work that I know is good, and why I am very careful about the guest blog posts I publish. (For example, I have turned down a fair amount of money that was offered to me to mention a blog-hosting company because I was asked not to disclose that it was a sponsored post. Not my thing). I have also turned down work because it doesn't match my personal ideals – most recently, writing copy for an e-cigarette website.

DO be human

If you have a personal presence on social media, and even if you only have a business presence, make sure that the person behind the business shows through. This applies especially if you're sharing your business posts on your personal account. I have a Libro Facebook page,[7] where I make sure you can see photos of me and ask for feedback as well as sharing my blog posts, and a personal page; I try to make sure I post more personal than business stuff on the personal page. People want to know the person behind the business, and they particularly don't want the friend they've followed to suddenly turn into a corporate mouthpiece.

DON'T bombard friends with your business message

It's very tempting to repost all of your business blog postings, etc. on to your personal Facebook and Twitter streams. It's even more tempting to shoehorn a mention of your business into every

---

[7] www.facebook.com/Libroediting

comment you make to your friends. We all know at least one person who does this (I've been accused of it myself by one person, but I do try hard to keep the balance), and what does it do? It puts you off buying their goods or service. Sorry, but it does. Do share your business stuff with your friends, but not at the expense of the normal friend stuff!

DON'T moan about your customers

This one is oh-so-tempting, too. Especially if you work alone, sometimes you have to MOAN. Here's the thing: moan, but don't do it in public. Really, don't. If you only follow one of these tips, follow this one. If you moan about a customer, even "just" on your personal Facebook timeline, how many of your friends might have been going to recommend your services to a friend, and might now be inclined not to? It's unprofessional.

Of course, we do all need to moan, but this is what you do: do it in private. I set up a local homeworkers' support group and an "Editors' Rah and Argh" group on Facebook – as private, invitation-only groups. If we want to roar, sob or moan, we do it there, or in an email to a friend, or in a cafe – not in public!

DON'T talk about your customers at all, actually

Not only the moaning, but be careful what you say about your clients in public. I have Non-Disclosure Agreements with some of mine, which means no talking, ever, but even with the others, I do not identify them by name when talking in public or writing about them in my book. I don't Tweet to my music journalist clients, outing myself as their transcriber, unless they specifically mention it in public first. I don't put their comments on my references page and CV before asking first. It's just good practice.

DON'T let people see the frantic paddling, just the serene swan

Cash flow problems or upset by something? I might mention in the most general terms that I'm feeling a bit stressed, but I usually won't. Although it's good to talk things out, if you run a business, you don't know who is watching. If you would be worried if a customer or prospect saw what you were writing, do it privately – create a filter or a private group on Facebook. If in doubt, don't talk about it in public.

DO be appropriate

If you manage rock bands and hang out at heavy metal festivals, by all means swear a bit on your public tweets. If you earn your living editing, try not to have spelling mistakes and typos all over your blog. (This is really hard to do – I know. Collect a group of friendly people who will let you know privately if such a thing occurs.) I lead a pretty quiet life, but I do try not to swear or have inappropriate pictures of me all over social media. Obviously that's easier the older you are and the less of your adult life has been lived in the full glare of social media, but you can always politely ask people to untag you from that hen party pic or horrendous shot from your younger days. If you explain politely that your business is linked to your name, and you're worried about affecting it, most people will surely comply with that. You can also untag yourself from Facebook posts and pictures and set up your profile so that you have to approve all tags, if you're at all worried.

My golden rule for maintaining a good online reputation

This is my golden rule. I've stuck by it ever since I started having an online presence:

Never say anything in public online that you wouldn't be happy shouting out loud in the middle of Birmingham [insert your own town or city as applicable].

SOCIAL CAPITAL – BUILDING AND BENEFITTING

How to leverage your social capital

How to leverage your social capital, eh? What a lot of jargon! I thought you didn't like jargon, Liz? – Well, I don't, and that's why I'm going to take a few minutes to explain what this little chunk of jargon means.

Social capital is a fancy term for the people you know and, to be blunt, the favours they owe you. You build it up through networking, doing things for other people, being a linking person, an information provider, a helpful person. You build it through knowing people, through having worked with people, through keeping in touch with people. Then, when you need it, something like karma springs into action, and the work you've put in comes back to you in bucketloads.

Now I'm sounding cynical as well as jargon-filled! Goodness me! Let's break it down with some heavily disguised but based-on-reality examples, to show you that leveraging your social capital isn't really the cynical and shallow procedure you might imagine, but a new name for an old process that is made easier by social media and our networked society.

Social capital gets leveraged, everyone goes away happy

Here are some examples of people leveraging their social capital to gain freelance jobs and repeat clients. Note that in NONE of these cases does Person A directly ask for something. Instead, the connections they've built up do it all for them.

Example 1

Bob "meets" John online via an online group for graphic designers. Bob is about to go full-time with his freelance career but doesn't have many clients. John is a full-time freelancer with a few more years' experience. He's looking for people to recommend enquirers on to when he can't fit them in and is also keen to get some holiday cover set up so he can go and play golf without worrying about his graphic design clients. They make friends and build trust – they even start to meet up to play golf together.

When John gets yet another enquiry about leaflet design, it's easy for him to recommend Bob. Bob worries sometimes that all of his jobs come through John's recommendations, but soon he has his own string of client referrals because he does a good job. And when Bob goes on holiday, he passes John a big project that he hasn't got time for – from a client originally recommended by John!

Who benefits? Both of them. Bob gets new clients and builds his customer base. John has people he can refer clients on to and that all-important holiday cover.

Bonus social capital leverage: when Bob, now nice and busy himself, finds out that a friend he's made at a networking event is looking for clients, not only can he recommend his own overflow to Tony, but he can advise John to, as well!

Example 2

Millie used to work with Jeremy before they both left MegaCorp Ltd. and went their separate ways. But they've kept in touch via Facebook and chat online every month or so. Jeremy moves between jobs and continents, so knows lots of people. When he hears from Simon, an ex-colleague in Australia, that they're looking for someone with the skillset Millie possesses, and that they don't need someone on the spot, Jeremy puts Millie in touch with Simon, and they work on the project together.

Who benefits? Both of them. Millie gets a job out of it, and Jeremy maintains contact with ex-colleagues and does them a favour, which could well be repaid in the future.

Example 3

Tim meets Shona at a local networking event. They're not in the same line of work at all, but they have a good chat and get on well. They say hello at a few other monthly events. One day, Tim is contacted by Sean, who wants to use him for a major new contract; he's been recommended by Shona, even though she has no direct experience of his work (of course, Sean has checked out Tim's website and references before contacting him). Not only does Tim get the job, but Sean recommends him on his website and to other clients of his.

Who benefits? In this case, it looks like it's mainly Tim. However, he is so grateful to Shona that he goes out of his way to retweet and share messages Shona sends out on social media, and to introduce her to useful people at the networking events they attend.

How to build social capital

So, how do you build this social capital? Note that it's not social MEDIA capital, although social media makes it easier to do. But you can build social capital through traditional networking and more old-fashioned face-to-face contact, too. In both Examples 2 and 3, the initial contact was in person, and social media only came into play to make the contacts between the people who want the work doing and lucky old Person A.

Building social capital shouldn't be a cynical process, but a natural one that involves making a bit of effort. Ways you can increase your social capital include:

Getting out there – the more people you meet, the more people can help you

Telling people what you're looking for – whether it's announcing to your Facebook friends that your violin-making business is looking for commissions, or joining a networking group and explaining what services or products you're promoting

Making yourself memorable – whether you're the "good hair lady" (true example) or the person who always brings cakes to the meetup, make yourself memorable in a good way

Making yourself easy to explain – this comes down to your elevator pitch. Do people know you as "the man who makes violins on commission" or "that music chap"? The more precise your description, the more likely you are to have people sent your way who you can actually work with

Being gracious – if someone is introduced to you who you can't help (or with whom you're not interested in working), see if you can recommend them on, or have a chat anyway. You need to leave a positive impression on everyone you meet if you possibly can

Do things for other people – this should go without saying, but I'm going to say it

It's cynical to say that someone "owes you one", and it can be far more complex than that, but it can't be ignored: the more you help other people, the more they will help you in return. How can you do things for other people?

If they're in the same business as you, see if you can pass overflow work to them

If they're in a closely related business to you, mention them to your clients as someone who can help them – e.g. the violin maker might know a musicians' agent who they can recommend to their clients

If they're in a fairly different business to you, bear them in mind and mention them – e.g. the violin maker might be chatting to a musician and mention that he knows an event organiser who's looking for entertainment for a summer party

If they're in a completely different business to you, still bear them in mind and suggest them – e.g. the violin maker might end up chatting to a musician whose wife needs a web page to be designed

You could create a Links page on your website with links to known and trusted contacts in your field and others

You could put a poster for their event in your shop window, or volunteer at an event they run

You could introduce a friend with a different kind of business to one of the networking events you go to

You could share tweets and Facebook posts by your contacts with your audience (you should be doing this anyway)

You could cross-guest-post on each other's blogs

CONCLUSION

Thank you for reading this far! Hopefully you've learned a few new things about using networking – whether physical networking in a room or social media networking online – to support and grow your business, including lots of tips about how to engender reciprocity and then leverage that social capital to gain advantage yourself AND to help others.

I've grown pretty much my entire business through social media and word of mouth (which is just a plain way of saying "social capital") and I hope that this guide will help you to do the same, saving some money and getting the nice, warm glow of having done something for yourself, and at no cost (apart from the time spent doing it).

If you've enjoyed this book, please do take a moment to review it on Amazon, Smashwords, Goodreads, your own blog or anywhere else you fancy. Reviews really do make a difference. I read them all, and love to see feedback, especially when I've helped somebody and their business!

RESOURCE GUIDE

Here are the URLs for all of the free resources I've linked to in the text of this book.

Setting up a business Facebook page:

http://libroediting.com/2014/10/08/facebook-for-business-starting-out/

Deleting posts and banning users on Facebook:

http://libroediting.com/2014/10/13/how-do-i-delete-a-post-or-ban-a-user-on-a-facebook-page/

Setting up a business Twitter page:

http://libroediting.com/2014/07/16/using-twitter-for-your-business/

Searching for jobs on Twitter:

http://libroediting.com/2013/12/23/searching-for-jobs-on-twitter/

Setting up a business LinkedIn page:

http://libroediting.com/2014/04/09/using-linkedin-for-your-business/

Setting up a business Google+ page:

http://libroediting.com/2014/10/22/google-for-business/

Setting up your WordPress blog:

http://libroediting.com/2014/01/03/wordpress-blog-basics/

General resource page with social media resources:

http://libroediting.com/blog/students-small-businesses-word-users

Growing your business:

http://libroediting.com/2013/11/25/developing-your-business/

ABOUT THE AUTHOR

Liz Broomfield (the pen name of Liz Dexter) is an editor, transcriber, proofreader and localiser based in Birmingham, UK. She's passionate about sharing the lessons she's learned as someone who changed careers mid-life and is living a flexible and happy life doing work she loves, with time for the other things she loves in life.

Liz's books can be found on Amazon, Smashwords and Selz in print and all formats of e-book.

Visit Liz's book website at
www.lizbroomfieldbooks.com

Visit Liz's business and Word tips website at
www.libroediting.com

ABOUT MY BOOKS

I write books that help self-employed people and people setting up and running small businesses to work out what to do first and what to do next. I write from my own experience, using lots of examples from my successful business life, and my books are all jargon-free, approachable and friendly. Most importantly, if you buy the book, you get the information that's promised. There's no requirement to buy a course or pay for additional materials. In fact, links and footnotes will take you to more FREE resources on my websites with screen shots and the latest updates. Find information, news and links to buy at www.lizbroomfieldbooks.com. Happy reading!

"How I Survived my First Year of Full-Time Self-Employment: Going it Alone at 40" – all you need to know about setting up your new business and taking the plunge without too much risk or anxiety. Lots of personal stories and I share exactly how I did it – you don't need to buy any courses or additional resources to get the full value from this book.

"Running a Successful Business after the Start-up Phase or, Who are you Calling Mature?" – you've set up the business, you've been running for a couple of years, now it's time to refine your customer base, redress your work-life balance and think about add-ons like social media networking and blogging. This book tells you how and like its predecessor, shares real-life examples which show exactly how I've built a happy self-employed life for myself.

The business OMNIBUS "Your Guide to Starting and Building your Business" – why not save money on buying the above two books separately with this e-only guide to setting up and maintaining a successful and balanced business? I do like to provide value to my readers, and this includes the text of both books in full, put together in a special omnibus edition. It's downloadable in all of the different e-book formats or as a pdf to read on your computer or tablet.

"How I Conquered High Cholesterol Through Diet and Exercise" – my first e-book and still one of the most popular, this takes you through what high cholesterol means, which foods make it worse and which might improve it, and places you might like to try eating, including restaurant tips for the UK and US. Built from my own experience, this offers an option for reducing cholesterol without drugs.

www.ingramcontent.com/pod-product-compliance
Lightning Source LLC
Chambersburg PA
CBHW021409170526
45164CB00002B/576